Transcript of the Unnamed

Transcript of the Unnamed

Poems by

Kateema Lee

Cover design by Shay Culligan

ISBN: 978-1-952326-40-0

Kelsay Books
502 South 1040 East, A-119
American Fork, Utah, 84003

To the missing, ignored, murdered, quiet, loud, hopeful, depressed, happy, strong, flawed, persistent women of color. We exist.

Acknowledgments

Many thanks to all of the editors and journals, in which some of these poems originally appeared.

Gargoyle: "Growing Up DC"

African American Review: "Hedera," "poem where we are fireflies," "poem where we are butterflies," "Epistle from a Missing Woman," and "Lost and Turned Out"

PMS: PoemMemoirStory / Nelle: "Legacy"

Beltway Poetry Quarterly: "Her Mythology," "Black Random," "Growing Up DC: Requiem," "Elegy for Chocolate City" and "Revisionist Musings"

Takoma Voice: Elegy for My Sister

Toe Good Poetry: "Taraxacum"

The Baltimore Review: "Transcript of the Unnamed"

SWIMM Every Day: "Heart Like Rambo"

Matter Press: Compressed Journal of Creative Arts: "hard light"

Eunoia Review: "Her Body," "Empty Nest"

The Sligo Journal: "On Defiance and Resisting"

This is What America Looks Like: Poetry and Fiction from DC, Maryland, and Virginia: "Last Epistle"

Contents

I

"the little girl is the world"

Growing Up DC

On Lebaum street in winter
a dog steals a little girl's gloves

kids slide down hills
on cardboard sleds

sand and snow slush under galoshes
the little girl cries

her big sister
tries to chase the dog

tries to temper chaos
for a moment the little girl loses

sight of her sister
the world is small

the world starts at Lebaum
and ends at Martin Luther King Avenue

the little girl is small
the little girl is the world

to her sister
the world is the little girl

to passersby
the girl stands on the sidewalk

in a world where dogs
take the little things

and leave a small part of her bare
while others take what they can

downward
inertia

the world
the little girl waits

and watches while everyone
around her moves

Hedera

Her family grew,
stretched from soil
to trellis to brick.

She was in there
somewhere, leaf
clinging to thin

stem, holding
to vine, welcoming
heat but avoiding

direct light. She knew
too much sun burned
layers, browning

so deep stems
would break off,
separating her from

familiar. So she grew
welcoming shade,
reaching up to

roof, touching
gutter, traversing
wood and dried clay,

reaching for bird
birth sky.

Legacy

I was born of Virginia Slims and sin.
My mother jokes that I came out
smelling like menthols and crying
Marvin Gaye's "Inner City Blues."

My mother was born of leaving.
Her father left after war and warring streets,
her mother, the queen of Hartford projects,
lived on highballs, was absent between bottles.

My father was born of church and Sunday dinners.
He says his nearly white mother sang "Precious Lord,
take my hand…," but she hated his pale skin, his godless
green eyes, his hatred for Sunday dinners.

His father, silent for years, died without saving him.
My father left when I was ten and God left
soon after. In church I was told that earth's
soil births bloom and seed.

Is it legacy to carry absence in harvest baskets,
to toss shovel and spade, to continue to dig
fingers deep into arid soil, hoping to sow
and grow something when nothing takes hold?

Queen of Hartford Street

Most visits I would follow Mom's boyfriend as he stuttered
and stutter-stepped up to my grandmother's apartment.

Three floors, his thin frame laboring
up sta-sta-stammering up,

up metal steps in a haze of alcohol, car exhaust
from his walk to the liquor store weighing

on his vocal chords. With his one hand holding a brown
paper bag, his other calloused hand gripping

the metal rail. Each step, a labor of breath, each step
an averted accident, a well-timed two-step,

st-st-steep steps, his wavy, black hair shining from sun
and sweat. E-E-Emma echoed each time he entered

the door, echoed in the hallway of the newly painted
project, echoed up until the slam of the steel door.

Each time he entered the door, Moms would cuss
him out, copy his stutter, hit him, full weight

behind her fist. Linwood limped through her apartment,
"E-E-Emma please." Moms, was the queen. She'd sit

by the window overlooking concrete courtyard,
watching me and the kids of her subjects play.

Sometimes my mother would do her hair, a rusty red
bouffant, Moms' crown. Each visit, Linwood would approach

her throne, leaving a gift wrapped in brown paper bag.
Each visit, my mother heated the hot comb. Each visit,

I watched Lindwood step through the door, watched Moms
punish the insolent, watched my mother try to please the queen.

Her Mythology

Like a hawk guarding its nest,
Moms sat surveying the courtyard
on Hartford Street. Elbow resting
gently on windowsill. She'd sit
night after summer night watching
children play and addicts stumble up
and down steps, watching them go inside
one of many metal doors. It's said
she was hit by lightning once, bolt
zeroing in on her third-floor apartment
window, zapping her down to the bone,
confirming her invincibility, changing
her brown hair root to end red.

"Lost and Turned Out"

after the Whispers

When we went food shopping, my mother would
wear blue eye shadow and heels that click-clacked up
and down grocery store aisles. Like Miss America waving
at each smiling admirer, she'd nod her head

and grin demurely while looking for Tide,
while selecting cabbage, canned Salmon, and greens,
while flirting with the men in the deli;
she had many male friends I could never call daddy.

On Sundays, when we were Jehovah's witnesses,
she would never play Ray Goodman and Brown
or the Whispers; she wouldn't sing Olivia,
one of her favorite Friday night songs, a song
she said she hoped I'd never understand.

I thought it was a song about Red Riding Hood;
I thought the most sinister wolves who
wore sheep's clothing hid shiny, soft coats beneath
wool and their teeth were more for smiles than bites.
My older sister came to understand that song.

On Fridays my mother would hum *break the chains
stop using your body and use your brain.* My older sister
would come home late. She never shopped with us
or prayed; I imagined she was Red Riding Hood laughing
with wolves, baying at the moon, never wearing
blue eye shadow and heels.

Elegy for My Sister

In the park a red bird caged in dead branches
sits still almost frozen enclosed
in a space of nature's creation.
The elements welcome it by melting
snow, slowing wind, raising the sun
just enough to warm its wings.
Below it on the ground crocuses
blossom, some with a strong purplish hue,
the creek nearby claps quietly against the rocks,
and *all feels right in the world*—right?
But, somewhere deep in the District
my sister haunts hallways and vacant lots,
never taking flight; sand, cement,
and abandoned cars her perch.
She sleeps in high-rise catacombs,
hollow spaces layered in rust,
cold dark places welcome her and others
searching for atonement,
apparitions to their families now.
Many are forgotten, never mourned,
just bones, then dust, talents never known.
My sister was an artist—
She'd sketch every new face she'd see,
shaping eyes, shading noses,
that's how I remember her now,
full tablets with charcoal images,
paints and faint memories of what
it was like to have an older sister.
I never could understand addiction,
nothing ever held me like that.

Theocratic Ministry School

This is where you learn how to teach others
about God. Your training starts early on cold
Saturday mornings, knocking on doors, smiling
while offering tools to salvation and the Watchtower
and Awake. You try to hide how much the wind hurts
and how much you don't know about Jehovah,
the world. You are barely old enough to reach
the doorbell, but He grants you the strength to reach
far enough to push. On Wednesdays, you sit
at a table on the stage in your dress, slip
showing for all to see. You open the book
to Corinthians and preach about *bad*
association spoiling useful habits.
From time to time, you look for your mother's face
in the sea of congregation. You want her to save you
but she smiles her prideful smile. You try to not think
about the nights she came home late, the times
you begged her to stay, the times you tried to save her.

Erasure

My mother mourned my sister
by raising her children. Each time
my sister had a child, my mother
read the bible and prayed.
When my sister abandoned them,
my mother took them in. One, two, three,
four, five, six versions of my sister
ended up in my mother's home.
I became the older sister,
babysitting, battling babies
for my mother's time. My space
wasn't filled but removed, as though I
had disappeared between bible verses.

Apetala1

her mother checked
brownness of ears.

She was relieved
to see more pink

than dark almond
or caramel, shade

as important
as fingers, toes.

There are pictures
somewhere: before

fallen petals and buds
failed to bloom,

before habits rooted
deeper than the oldest tree,

before the threat
of being uprooted,

photos of a girl, sepals accepting
rain like a mother's love.

Learning

A little girl walks
behind her mother.
Her lesser footsteps
trying to match
her mother's rhythm.
For every step
her mother takes,
she takes two.

she carries…

her mother's voice,
low hum of undertow.
some hear the nuance,
question the tone;
sounds bounce
on tympanic; others
lose their way
in cochlea.
this is their shared
echo, to be heard
from disparate
frequencies. there's bass
where gravitas hits
membrane. the hollow
mumbling, survival's chords

II

"to some, survival is luxury"

Away from Home

She's a community college student
sitting with an older man. She's young,
and white. When the older man leaves

for a restroom break, a young waiter
approaches the table. She, nervously giggling,
tells him she's majoring in nursing. He tells

her his major is finance; he wants to work
on Wall Street. They share pleasantries
in whispers. She says she wants weed

and fun. She does not like Rhode Island;
she misses home. He gives her his number.
I laugh at this transaction. My back to them,

I can't see their faces but I've seen
their faces, and for a moment, I try
to imagine what it's like to be young

and woman and oppressed, as all women
are oppressed, and beautiful and free
to ask for whatever I want but to know

that my body is currency and gateway
to freedom or weed or whatever freedom
looks like these days in my young skin,

but what does this brown middle-aged body
know? I have no idea what it means
to be free in that way.

All I know is the overcooked marlin
in front of me, the nonalcoholic cocktail
commingling with ice and lemon wedge. I know

invisibility in public spaces, and the self-
imposed weight of the world, the weight of real
and imagined. I know of busy

mashed potatoes and sautéed spinach.
I know what my well-traveled friends
would call trivial problems:

having to pay for solitude.
I know this meal, the imported sparkling
water in a long-stemmed glass.

Calochortus: Squaw Valley

after Robert Hass

Through the window, vertical blinds slice up
the village, mountains daring to be moved.
She wants to take footholds, fold the mountain
pocket-sized, take it with her to Anacostia.
She wants to transport lavender valleys, Mariposa lilies,
and snow-capped peaks, to slowly unfold rock, slopes,
and tall, thin trees that lean like lanky men,
but she wants to revise, before creases form, leave
elevator whispers and people walking
along pseudo-cobblestone. Someone
describes her as immigrant. Her partner,
 settled in green fields they nurture to hold them, says
 don't be exhausted; just find some cool spots
for us to invade. Sometimes, they find windy plateaus,
crosspollinate, then leave. But this space is a bulb
that has failed to open. She is new to this place
on purpose, but she is not new to This place,
sitting in houses with Native statues
and tribal headdresses. Antler sconces
and antler chandeliers poke holes in narrative
photos of happy fiction riding ski lifts;
Over and over she's told it's dry here,
but there are wood beams, wood walls, wood decks.
She imagines melancholy trees and bears striking matches.
Trees are her totem. Her mother says she's blessed,
as she buzzes people in and out of new, waterfront
condos back home. Even now, the petals take the heat,
are sustenance to some; to some, survival is luxury.

Heart Like Rambo

At sixty-six, my mother can't retire. Most of her life
she saw risk as God's blessing. Married over and over,
moved here, there, and back. Back in the day,
she was power, afro swag, wearing platform boots.

Today, she wears a uniform, helps "important people"
enter buildings. She complains she doesn't have much.
I remind her she is rich in other ways. I'm not my mother.
My only risk is flying; I revel in that feeling after the fasten

seatbelt sign is off, the exhaling after unbuckling, the stretch
of legs, the sway of hips up and down the aisle, a freedom
fear strangles on land. Is it possible to feel blessed and broken?
Some of us hold onto safety like deeply planted roots hold onto soil.

My 80s-loving friend says high altitude makes hearts
strong like Rambo. To my friend, it makes sense to always be alert,
always protecting self. He understands the need to fortify during
peacetime, to prepare, to build a fortress. We build forts

around each other sometimes, send Morse code distress signals
 at "first blood." Most times, we exchange pleasantries,
then disappear. In another life, we would've been lovers
planting landmines for anyone unlucky enough to find

our refuge. But risk? At sea-level loneliness is an anchor.
My mother never hesitates to "put God to the test."
Some of us are trees trying to retire trunk heavy.

Normalcy 2000s

Las Vegas was breaking news; a country concert, cowboy boots
decorated with stars and stripes rest in the street; pay cell bill;
Puerto Ricans, palms drowning; a little boy eats candy and smiles
at the camera; grocery list piling up: eggs, juice, toilet paper,
tampons; another black man shot; NFL players arm and arm or on
their knees; Jerry Jones struggles to stand, and some fans say *keep
politics out of my sports*. A black woman is missing. ~~save~~ football.
Somewhere unarmed black shot. Dry cleaning ready for ~~rescue~~
pickup; find the ransom note. Two women stabbed in Marseille.
Not acid this time. Clean, vacuum the clusters of cat hair
suffocating threads of Persian rug, dust the ceiling fan so it can
breathe. He said, *I can't breathe*. Tiki torch memes on Twitter. Take
supplements. Another church shooting. The suspect, they say, was
a member. Pray. She was last seen near water. Pay cable bill,
mortgage, car note, cancel Equifax subscription. The stock market
is doing well, *despite uncertainty* they say on CNBC. New
neighbors paid above market. The gunman was a senior living in a
well-kept home. She was in her cell. "What drives a man to do
such a thing," Brian Williams asks. Pandemic zooms in. Time to
wear another mask. Checks items off the list.

Empty Nest

after Aliens

"Get away from her you bitch," Ripley yells;
Newt calls her mommy. Ripley becomes

pyromaniac mama, protecting her young.
Every time she cradles Newt's young, fragile

body, ovaries dance like they are futile fertile,
free to reproduce like the rapid fire of her pulse rifle.

Older bodies fight confusion, play dirty
pre-gray tricks at the site of maternal.

Even as the xenomorph queen lays her eggs,
breast engorge with imaginary milk.

As Ripley sprays the queen's nest and each egg burns,
we think about loss and how even in the movies,

someone else decides whose children will live or die

and how choice is flammable and how some women
are happy to hand out matches, to watch

possibility burn. As Ripley grips Newt
and waits for Bishop, we watch the flames.

Taraxacum

Sometimes I forget I'm black, despite my brown,
moley and freckled face. Sometimes
when I look in the mirror I only see
an aging woman. When asked to describe myself,

I say average. Sometimes my students
laugh at me. Sometimes I pretend to be
someone else. Sometimes when I walk the halls
at home, at work, at the mall, I'm more interested

in the click-clack of my footsteps. But one day
when driving through my neighborhood and seeing
three little brown girls, their heads florets
of plaits, pigtails, and barrettes, leaning into

the passenger window of a police car—
three little girls innocently giggling,
talking to someone who's vowed to be impartial,
to defend, nothing menacing in that scene,

I felt afraid. At that moment, I remembered
being nine or ten, learning that to some
I was cute for a brown girl and to others
I was no more than a weed needing to be pulled,

discarded like the "Freeway Phantom" girls. I remembered
how I worked in my grandmother's garden, how I picked
dandelions first because I wanted to save them,
how I loved their beautiful, bright heads hiding

from no one, finding stages in cracked cement.
At that moment in my car, held by sinister
innocence, I was afraid for their brown bodies,
hallow stalks, dancing in place. Few will mourn

those girls or when they are women welcome
their achenes balleting in the wind
or mourn those deeply rooted in addiction's soil.
At that moment, I wanted to save those girls;

instead, I watched like a concerned mother peeking
out the screen at her kids playing outside.
I wanted to call out to them;
I wanted to tell them to come home.

Remembrance

¹for six D.C. girls, 1971-1972

She grew up hearing about girls
who never made it to womanhood, girls
whose names wore away with each decade,
girls who walked the same streets

she walked some days and nights,
at times for something to do,
at times for food, at times to just go
somewhere, but she always made

it home. As she grew, fertile
fields grew into cautionary tales
and strength. This is what some
girls do before they are women.

They disappear. They disappear. They disappear.

They are grains in the air, left floating
in afternoon, evening, and night breezes,
settling like ghost on retinas.

---

¹ Carol Spinks, Darlenia Johnson, Brenda Crockett, Nenomoshia Yates, Brenda Woodward, Diane Williams

III

"Her mother… would break the world"

Transcript of the Unnamed

You better bet that if these had been white girls, the police would have solved the cases.
                    —Evander Spinks, a sister of the first Freeway Phantom victim

I.

We are told we are

daughters of Ham,

and we carry his sins

in our womb.

Each birth

unearths another,

like us, destined

to be punished.

II.

They were chosen

at random. He saw them

walking. That's all

it took, a brilliant,

brown body walking

to the store, fragile

as fireflies in wind.

All he had to do

was open his jar,

tilt it ever so slightly

to add another one

to his collection.

III.

In the District on the A bus,
a little girl asks—*"if I disappear,*
would anyone look for me?" Her mother,
wearing long cornrows and pride,
tells her child she would break the world,
turn over buses and buildings, knock down
the Big Chair to find her. The girl smiles,
squeezes her mother's hand, waits
for her turn to pull the cord.

IV.

Daughters of Ham wearing church hats pray
their babies come home safe, that God bless
the child lost to the streets, the child left
like trash on the side of the road, the child
who is one of four with a mother
who is still a child. They pray on Sundays
as the organ plays, their faith safe between
clasped hands. The say *amen and hallelujah.*
With the wisdom of oracles, they sing hymns
to unburden their souls and the souls
of those to come, kneeling in prayer, hands
so tight even loss couldn't break the seal.

We Carry

after Niki Giovanni's "Cotton Candy on a Rainy Day"
& Lucille Clifton's "homage to my hips"

To be born a girl and brown is to be born between joy
and bruise. Some of us learn to carry calm and grief
in name-brand bags and in tight crossways of cornrow;
some walk around with a don't mess with me smile;

some carry the blues passed down from sinners
and saints, small breaches in rhythm wearing
away mask after mask, losing beats between hits.
Some of us sing between bills, between babies,

between absence and loss, between wigs, loosening
threads and burned ends, between lovers of big butts
and the ones who praise everyone's round hips but ours.
Sometimes we are like worn nonstick surfaces; we burn

anything that touches unprotected seams. Some of us learn that
love, at times, is a fist waiting to find a place to plant, and living
can be cotton candy on a rainy day.

We learn to savor and save the sweet, to make sugary, melting
threads respites of joy, to dance as what's left washes away.

Her Body

after Colin Garland's Sable Venus
& Lucille Clifton's "Homage to My Hips"

Eyes avert from the sight of her form,
from the shape of her waist to the curve
of her thighs, her *free hips* crafted in the image

of man's imagination of God's imagination
of woman. There's a rush to clothe her
in her imagined shame, some parts

still a cloth-covered guarded secret. Each time
some part of her is exposed, many are outraged,
afraid of what may come, afraid of what it means

to be bare and unafraid. As white Venus rises
from the foam, her body exposed to eyes
and elements, no one looks away

and viewers praise the brilliance of the sea,
but the breasts of a brown body
leads to the fear that comes

with not wanting to look, but looking anyway,
like a *wardrobe malfunction* during
a half-time show. Her uncovered breasts

welcome the wind and the gloss
of the sun. She is on her way to shore;
no one, god or mortal, can stop her.

hard light

by definition
she is an absence
little cut-out girl
with no lucent
light   the window
withholds natural
unforgiving
as angle of view
alone
blue-black form
purposeful
a shadow's silhouette
if removed would she
be missed   if kept
would she be missed
transcription
of the unnamed
if lit   named If
would she become
a focal figure
muddy contrast
origin fixed

Anacostia Girls

after Shakespeare's Sonnet 60

We are cormorants kissing   white waves, upturned wings

worshiping the sky. *As the waves*   *make towards the coast…*

so do our minutes hasten   *to their end;* We fly or die.

She Go-Go

Her   body   moves

        to   conga   drums;
hips   rhythm   bounce

to   hi-hats   call
     and   cowbells   chant.

         She   dances   cised
     to   Black Holes'   funk;
teen   bodies   sweat
     to   Go-Go   swing.

No   bullets   yet,
     no   bamas   touch,
     no   phantom   girls,
        or   southeast   threat.

     She   dances   youth,
while   Chuck Brown   plays;

     no   highway   end,

        just   Go-Go's   sway.

poem where we are fireflies

He pulls wings off fireflies;
whimsically catching them,
he jumps victoriously in the air,
cupping his hands together, jailing
them between his palms; he marvels
at their light, how their brilliance
disappears then reappears between
tight grip and blinks; it is said
we are endangered, losing battle
after battle to his innocent hands,
only surviving long enough
to light each other's path.

Epistle from a Missing Black Woman

When you file the report,
tell them my eyes are unsolved cases,
my mouth a missing woman,
my head, disembodied,
Charon's middle finger. The cross-
ways of Acheron my hair.
The building blocks of my face
are tragedy at first glance.
My neck can hold the weight
of the Atlantic.

Sincerely,
[Unnamed]

poem where we are butterflies

sometimes we find ourselves in places
where flowers hide their bloom;

sometimes, we don't know
the difference between

pungent rot or honeyed
sunflower or spring garden

or window flowerpot; we live to land
on something, wings fluttering,

to leave atoms of self behind,
to repeat the cycle, to live a brief, bright life.

"Sign o' the Times"

Like Prince, she prayed to Jehovah, her faith at times
wavering between the bible and grandma's gospel.

When discussing addiction, her mother
says, "some people don't have a bottom."

There are news tickers missing names. Yesterday,
her name was crisis. There are named nameless women.

Even bees tread water, wings heavy between waves;
sometimes she forgets to fly.

If mortals can make chairs for giants and monuments
for gods, she believes she can survive the times.

On the news, she saw plastic rings littered along the Anacostia;
for a brief moment she couldn't breathe.

What does it mean when she has to refuse blood
to show faithfulness to god?

Her good girlfriends say, "ain't nobody checkin'
for black women." Some things are gospel.

On Defiance and Resisting

My father was an imposing man;
most times he used his size to intimidate.
Like Goliath to David, he forced men

and women to stand in his shadow,
to feel the cold shade of his presence.
But I never cowered. My seemingly

fragile frame hid the strength of Amazons.
From my father I learned to never fear
men or fear the loss of light some may bring,

or the dark that comes when a man stands,
like my father, to force uneasiness.
Defiance is meeting every giant eye to eye,

without focusing on arms or hands threatening
to limit. Defiance is not letting the death of a woman
who blew smoke in the face of a smaller

giant break you or to lose your courage
to the truth that even young or aging
bodies will never be safe in a world

where confiscating rocks and slings trump
everything. Resisting is living between
the pendulum of elegance and a shotgun in the face.

Last Epistle

If I die suspiciously, please know
I didn't kill myself. If you read
my statuses, emails and tweets,
testimonies to tiresome days and anti-
climactic nights, know I knew life
was more tepid creek than volcano.
I wouldn't jog my daily route then dive
into dark water, and if by chance I fell in,
I would grow gills. I wouldn't shape
ropes out of bags or dare any savior
to take my life.
                        Melancholy
is not preface to death. Black or brown
is not prologue to demise. My birth
is not precursor to my passing
too soon. If I disappear,
look for me.

Sincerely,
[Unnamed]

Black Random

I am sitting on a bus. My ears are the same
shade they were at birth. I am sitting on a train.

The sun has claimed my face and arms. The seats
near me are canyons only mules cross. Freckles

and moles are roadmaps to my age. I am sitting
in my car. My sex is aubergine in day.

It changes with the season. People honk
when I sit seconds at green lights. The sun

assaults my arm resting in the window.
I am stopped by siren. My hands and knuckles

tell tales. They are well-worn gloves gripping
wheel. My headlights are bold; my phoropter

adjusts to shades and situations. I am sitting
on a plane. The rows show hints of history.

My iris is narrative. I'm encoded
on retinas. I am sitting in my car,

black random, next to a curb on a busy street
hoping for reprieve. I am home. My body

is hairless summer sitting in the tub white-
washed from the day, welcoming the night.

Revisionist Musings

The statue of liberty
is on her knees folding a flag.
She's tired of the pattern.

Abraham Lincoln owns
a national football team
called the The Emancipators.

Betsy Ross has a makeup
line showcasing shades
of red, white, and blue.

Robert E. Lee has a prize-
winning rose garden. He sends
fresh cut flowers to Harriet Tubman.

Thomas Jefferson is engaged
to George Washington. They
are registered at Tiffany & Co.

Martin Luther King plays golf
during hurricanes. His handicap
is low when it rains.

Presidents live in projects
like Garfield Hills or Barry Farms.
They sign laws in ice cream trucks.

Words like [redacted] and [redacted]
are less painful than tight cornrows
or tightly sewn yaki weave.

Mayonnaise is as flavorful as watermelon.
Breadcrumbs belong on mac and cheese.
Chef Ramsey cooks grits on Sundays.

America's pastime is reading *The Souls
of Black Folk.* Twitter and Facebook are birds
in gilded cages singing gospel songs.

Elegy for Chocolate City

for D.C.

Her city used to be sweet, dark
luxury, but some streets were sour,

known for their bitter taste.
Her city was sublet, many names

on the lease; native nonnatives;
her name was clinched fist.

Her city was ambassador of Quan.
Quan lived on MLK near the asylum.

Some seek asylum from politicians'
wet dreams, dreams of sitting on top

a hill, a hill too high for people like her
to climb, a climb with a steep decline,

a decline steeper than rent, rent subsidized
by bodies and grime, grime at the bottom

of basins. The Basin is not far from Lincoln;
Lincoln freed the slaves, and slaves built

the city; the city built slaves and placed
them in projects; projects were night;

night's soundtrack was bullets;
Bullets changed their name to Wizards;

Wizards did not cast spells or grant wishes;
some wished for mambo sauce on wings.

Wings were needed things in her city,
so needed she tried to fashion them from loss.

Growing Up DC: Requiem

they ask me to remember
but they want me to remember
their memories and I keep on remembering mine
                    —*Lucille Clifton*

I.

In the nation's capital big chairs were made
for giants and monuments were made for gods.

Hinckley sat in St. Elizabeths and across the street
Aunt Rena cooked Cream of Wheat for Uncle George

in her first-floor apartment off Martin Luther King Ave.
In the alley, another somebody jumped.

                                                    II.

                    Away from the columns with acanthus
                leaves and the labyrinth of working masses
                    she's movah to three kids   she walks
            to the busstop erry morning to take one of her girls
                            to half-day kinneygarten
                    she sings   has six-inch nails
                            has yaki thick dreams
                        wants to sit in the Big Chair
                        wants to be a monument

III.

When growing up, fascinated with mountains,
volcanoes, ruins and planets,
her fascination was both earthly and otherworldly.

Her mind, neighborhood, house, or apartment
was linked to some mountainous place
perched so high she could see everything;

She could imagine all things;
Most times she would try to find
footholds not meant for climbing,

yet sometimes she climbed the grassy side,
admiring peaks and valleys, mud, looking
up at sky, cityscape oblivious. Monuments

had no meaning, capitals were what she learned
about in school, and chocolate city was a black hole,
go-go, bamas-better-not-play birth home

where no one but her family wanted life. She remembers a where
where ground swallowed people but left their heads
just enough above ground so they could breathe.

About the Author

Kateema Lee is a Washington D.C. native. Her recent work has been published in print and online journals such as Beltway Poetry Quarterly, African American Review, Gargoyle, Baltimore Review, and others. Kateema is the author of two chapbooks, *Almost Invisible* and *Musings of a Netflix Binge Viewer.*

www.ingramcontent.com/pod-product-compliance
Lightning Source LLC
Chambersburg PA
CBHW071358090426
42738CB00012B/3155